Shojin
Ryori

Mindful Japanese Vegetarian Cooking

Shojin Ryori

Danny Chu

Marshall Cavendish
Cuisine

To my gurus, 14th Dalai Lama Tenzin Gyatso, Drukpa Choegon Rinpoche, Lama Zopa Rinpoche, Lama Lhundrup and Geshe Chonyi, who have shown me great compassion and wisdom through their enlightened activities and teachings. Their blessings made all things possible.

In memory of my mum, Nancy, and my partner, Diamond — your love made me believe that dreams really, and do, come true. You will always be in my heart.

To my tabby cat, Gobo, who purrs me on till today.

About the Author

Danny Chu is a former foreign currency trader who left the corporate world and followed his passion to Japan to learn more about *shojin ryori*, the art of Japanese Zen cuisine. With hard work and unwavering determination, Danny mastered traditional Zen temple cooking and became the first *shojin ryori* chef in Singapore.

He ran Enso Kitchen for several years, delighting both vegetarians and non-vegetarians alike with his creative dishes, and garnered rave reviews from the media, including *Wine & Dine*, *Travel+Leisure*, *BBC Good Food*, *Appetite* and *The Peak* magazines, as well as *The Business Times* and Channel News Asia.

This is Danny's first cookbook. His second book is entitled *Living Shojin Ryori: Plant-based Cooking from the Heart*.

Currently based in Taiwan, Danny shares his love for *shojin* cooking through classes and demonstrations overseas.

Contents

Introduction

Shojin means vigour or energy and *ryori* means cuisine. Together, the term *shojin ryori* refers to the cuisine that originated from the Buddhist temples in Japan in the 6th century and which gained popularity with the introduction of Zen Buddhism in the 13th century.

Preparing *shojin* cuisine is an aspect of Zen training. It involves the cook's entire personality, not just his cooking skills, and is a practice of spirituality. It is an art of cooking which involves the delicate preparation of the ingredients, and where the cook has to be mindful of the cooking process, right up to the presentation of the dish.

Derived from the basic Buddhist precept of not taking life, *shojin ryori* is completely vegetarian. When preparing a *shojin ryori* meal, one key aspect is to minimise any wastage of ingredients, while drawing out the natural flavour of each ingredient.

Traditionally, the Zen Buddhist monks would chant and contemplate the five Zen reflections before eating:

The effort that brings me this meal
This is an appreciation of the effort made to put the meal together, from harvesting the crops, to preparing the ingredients and even those who made the tableware and cutlery. The meal is possible only through the kindness of others.

My imperfections as I receive this meal
This is the recognition that nobody is perfect, so the individual is kept humble and the heart open, thankful and appreciative of the goodness of life.

Mindfulness to be free from imperfections
This is to keep free from negativity through rightful actions, speech and thinking. Only when one is fully aware of his shortcomings, would he seek to change for the better.

Taking this food to sustain good health
The essence of this reflection is to be mindful of what one eats as food has an impact on health.

The fulfillment of our obligations
The essence of living is to achieve one's goals. With this in mind, the individual is able to uplift his spirits and reach his goals.

Simple, Delicious, Healthy

Shojin cooking uses seasonal ingredients to get the best out of the produce in order to nourish the body. The ingredients are purely vegetables or from plant sources, and no artificial colouring and flavouring is used. It also omits the use of eggs and dairy products, making it suitable for vegan diets.

Once, when I had the opportunity to visit a farm in Japan, I noticed how the farmer took a lot of pride in her work. To introduce me to the produce, she harvested a turnip from the ground, washed it and cut it in half for me to try. The turnip tasted sweet and mild, even though it was not even peeled. Seeing my surprise at how good the turnip tasted, the farmer commented that most vegetables taste good as they are. She then joked that as the chef needed a job, they started to make things more elaborate and created dishes.

This simple encounter made me realise the benefits of using seasonal produce, of enjoying vegetables when they are fresh and tasty. It is with this understanding that I have created and served many different seasonal *shojin* sets. Despite having done this for the past decade, I remain in awe at how these dishes can be prepared with such simple ingredients, yet be so delicious and healthy.

Shojin ryori is made up of a variety of dishes and presented on trays. Care and attention is given to the presentation, the colours and the taste to intrigue the five senses.

I have specially created the menus in this book using seasonal ingredients that can be easily found outside of Japan. In addition, I have also suggested substitutes for ingredients where applicable, so you will not be limited by the availability of ingredients.

The dishes can also be prepared and enjoyed individually, so you do not need to prepare the full set if you do not wish to. The important thing is for the experience to be light-hearted and peaceful. Enjoy!

Shojin Seasonal Menu

Although *shojin ryori* originated as a cuisine prepared by the Buddhist monks in the Zen temples as part of their spiritual practice, the essence of *shojin* cooking is about mindfulness and enjoyment. The recipes are relatively easy to follow and practical, and can be enjoyed by all.

There are no particular rules or sequences to follow in eating or serving the dishes in *shojin* cooking. Instead, the emphasis is placed on balance and harmony. And as such, different cooking methods, ingredients and flavours can be used to intrigue the senses when putting together a *shojin* meal.

In the following section, I have put together different menus based on the four seasons: spring, summer, autumn and winter. The recipes used seasonal items that could be found if you have access to Asian ingredients. Each season features two groups of five dishes, paired with the same soup and rice or noodle dish. For instance, the rice and soup on page 28 will be repeated on page 42. This is done deliberately for easy reference. While *shojin ryori* is often prepared as a set so that the meal is complete, it is perfectly fine to prepare just individual dishes.

Basic Preparations

This section consists of a number of basic preparations, such as rice, stocks and garnishes, which are required in Japanese cooking. You will find these basic preparations useful even when preparing other Japanese dishes.

The beauty of *shojin ryori* is that it does not require any special kitchen equipment. While I do highlight the use of a few Japanese kitchen tools in the recipes, it is only because these tools can make the job easier and save time and energy. They are however not essential and you can do without them.

JAPANESE RICE

Serves 4

220 g (8 oz) Japanese
short-grain rice

5-cm (2-in) konbu

270 ml (9 fl oz) water

Place rice in a bowl and fill with water from the tap.
Wash thoroughly by stirring briskly with your hand.
Discard cloudy water or set aside for other uses.
Repeat process until water is almost clear. Place rice in
a sieve to drain for 15 minutes. Transfer drained rice to
a bowl.

Use a clean damp cloth to wipe surface of konbu. Add
konbu and water to bowl of rice and leave to soak for
at least 30 minutes.

Pour contents of bowl into a rice cooker and cook rice
according to the manufacturer's directions. When rice
is ready, discard konbu and fluff up rice before serving.

The water from washing rice can be used to boil vegetables
or water plants in your garden. This is a *shojin* philosophy of
minimising wastage.

KONBU DASHI

Makes 1.25 litres (40 fl oz / 5 cups)

12-cm (5-in) konbu

1.25 litres (40 fl oz / 5 cups)
water

Use a clean damp cloth to wipe the surface of konbu.
Place konbu in a pot with water and leave to soak for
at least 2 hours.

Place pot over medium heat and bring water to the
boil. Lower heat and simmer for 10 minutes. Remove
konbu. The konbu dashi is ready to be used.

If you do not have the time to soak the konbu for 2 hours, a
quick way is to place the konbu in a pot with the water. Bring
to the boil, then lower heat and simmer for 20 minutes.

In *shojin* cooking, konbu dashi is a main stock that uses only
konbu for the soup base. Unlike most Japanese cooking,
bonito (fish flakes) are not added.

MUSHROOM DASHI

Makes 1.25 litres (40 fl oz / 5 cups)

8 dried shiitake mushrooms

1.25 litres (40 fl oz / 5 cups) water

Rinse mushrooms and place in a pot with water. Leave to soak for about 3 hours.

Remove mushrooms and gently squeeze the water back into the pot. The mushroom dashi is ready to be used.

Like konbu dashi, mushroom dashi is another stock that uses only one ingredient, in this case, dried shiitake mushrooms, for the soup base.

If you are pressed for time, the process can be shortened by simmering. Boil the water in a pot and add the rinsed mushrooms. Lower heat and simmer for 10–15 minutes. Remove mushrooms and set aside to cool. When cool, gently squeeze the water back into the pot. The mushroom dashi is ready to be used.

TOASTED and GROUND SESAME SEEDS

Sesame seeds, as needed

Place a frying pan over medium heat. Add sesame seeds and stir constantly.

When sesame seeds darken and take on a glossy sheen, remove from heat immediately.

Grind sesame seeds with a *suribachi* or mortar and pestle. Use as needed.

BOILED BAMBOO SHOOTS

Fresh bamboo shoots, as needed

Rice water (from rinsing rice), as needed

For every 3 litres (96 fl oz / 12 cups) rice water, use:

2 Tbsp raw sugar

1 tsp sea salt

Wash off any dirt and remove tough outer sheaths and root end of fresh bamboo shoots. Place in a pot.

Pour rice water into the pot to cover bamboo shoots. Add sugar and salt and bring to a boil. Lower heat and simmer for 1 hour or more until bamboo shoots are tender. Remove bamboo shoots from the pot and set aside to cool.

You should be able to peel off the remaining outer skin of the bamboo shoots easily. The bamboo shoots are now ready to be used.

Starter

GOMA DOFU (Sesame Tofu)
Serves 4

30 g (1 oz) *kuzu*

2 Tbsp white sesame paste

250 ml (8 fl oz / 1 cup) water

Ice cubes, as needed

Wasabi, to taste

SAUCE

3 Tbsp konbu dashi
(page 19)

3 Tbsp Japanese soy sauce

Start by preparing the sauce. Combine konbu dashi and soy sauce in a saucepan. Bring to a boil, then set aside to cool.

Mix *kuzu*, sesame paste and water together in a non-stick saucepan, stirring until the mixture is smooth. Place sesame mixture over medium heat. Stir vigorously and continuously with a sturdy wooden spatula for 10–15 minutes until mixture is thick. It should coat the spatula and not drip off rapidly when you scoop it up. Turn off the heat and continue to stir for another 2 minutes.

Rinse a 17.5 x 8 x 6-cm (7 x 3 x $2^1/_3$-in) metal tray with water and leave it wet. This will ensure that the *goma dofu* does not stick to the tray when set. Pour the sesame mixture into the tray. Level it out and pat the top with a spatula. Make sure there are no air bubbles. Place the tray on a low rack or on two small shallow dishes in a container filled with water. This will allow the water to circulate around and beneath the tray to cool the *goma dofu*.

Wet a muslin cloth and use it to cover the sesame mixture. Place some ice cubes in the tray and in the container of water to force-cool the *goma dofu*. Set aside for about 3 hours.

To unmould the *goma dofu*, place the tray under cold running water and run your finger along the edge of the *goma dofu*. Lift it out onto a large plate or chopping board.

Cut into 4 pieces and serve with the sauce and wasabi.

Do not put the *goma dofu* in the refrigerator to cool as it will harden and not have the desired texture.

If preparing a larger quantity, you may need to stir the mixture for a longer time until the sesame mixture is thick and coats the wooden spatula.

This dish is made without soy beans, but it is so-named for its tofu-like texture. This springy Japanese delicacy is known as the king of *shojin ryori* as it epitomises the spirit of *shojin* cooking, using the least amount of ingredients for maximum natural flavour. I have faithfully served this as a starter for all my *shojin* dining menus as it is a fitting introduction to *shojin ryori*.

Spring

Spring always gives me a sense of new beginning.
It is when the trees start to bud and flowers
start to blossom. In the spring menu that follows,
you will also notice that the dishes include
many fresh spring vegetables.

SHISO RICE

Serves 4

Japanese rice (page 19)

2 green shiso leaves

Prepare Japanese rice.

Remove and discard stems of shiso leaves. Wash and pat dry, then chop leaves finely and add to rice. Mix well and serve.

Shiso leaves have a distinctive taste. The finer it is chopped, the more intensive the flavour.

CLEAR VEGETABLE BROTH

Serves 4

1.25 litres (40 fl oz / 5 cups) mushroom dashi (page 20)

80 g (2⁴/₅ oz) carrot

100 g (3¹/₂ oz) daikon

2.5-cm (1-in) knob ginger

2 Tbsp sesame oil

3 Tbsp Japanese soy sauce

¹/₂ tsp sea salt

Prepare mushroom dashi and set aside.

Peel carrot and daikon. Cut each root vegetable into 8 chunky pieces. Peel ginger and cut into 3 or 4 slices.

Heat sesame oil in a pot and add ginger slices. Fry for about 1 minute. Add carrot and daikon chunks and cook until a little charred around the edges.

Add mushroom dashi, soy sauce and salt and bring to the boil. Lower heat and simmer for 15-20 minutes, skimming off and discarding any foam that rises to the surface from time to time.

Serve hot.

DAIKON ROLLS

Serves 4

120 g (4¹⁄₃ oz) daikon

Watermelon, as needed

Cucumber, as needed

8 sprigs coriander leaves (cilantro)

4 Tbsp toasted and ground sesame seeds (page 21)

CITRUS DRESSING

4 Tbsp orange juice

1 Tbsp lemon juice

2 Tbsp mirin

2 Tbsp rice vinegar

1 Tbsp raw sugar

¹⁄₃ tsp sea salt

1 tsp cornflour, mixed with 2 Tbsp water

Peel daikon and cut into half lengthwise. Using a vegetable slicer, cut daikon into thin slices, each about 10-cm (4-in) long. Make 8 such slices.

Cut watermelon into sticks, each about 5-cm (2-in) long and 1-cm (¹⁄₂-in) thick. Make 8 watermelon sticks.

Cut cucumber into sticks, each about 5-cm (2-in) long and 0.5-cm (¹⁄₄-in) thick. Prepare 16 cucumber sticks.

Prepare toasted and ground sesame seeds. Set aside.

To make citrus dressing, combine all ingredients except cornflour slurry in a saucepan and place over low heat. When mixture starts to boil, give cornflour slurry a stir and add to saucepan. Whisk to thicken dressing.

To assemble, place a watermelon stick, 2 cucumber sticks and a coriander stalk on each slice of daikon. Roll up and squeeze gently to help roll hold its shape. Dip one end of daikon roll in toasted and ground sesame seeds.

Arrange 2 daikon rolls on each dish. Serve with citrus dressing.

To make a pretty daikon roll, have the coriander hanging out at one end and coat the other end with sesame seeds.

The daikon rolls can be secured with some of the dressing or with a toothpick.

Raw daikon is used in Japan to counter
the taste of oily food. But more importantly, it has
enzymes that aid digestion. This recipe has an interesting
combination of various raw vegetables rolled into one,
served with a refreshing citrus-flavoured thick sauce.

PARBOILED SHUNGIKU
with DASHI SOY

Serves 4

300 g (11 oz) *shungiku* (chrysanthemum) leaves

$1/_2$ tsp sea salt

DASHI SOY

4 Tbsp konbu dashi (page 19)

4 tsp Japanese soy sauce

4 tsp mirin

Prepare konbu dashi and set aside until needed.

Rinse *shungiku* leaves well.

Boil a pot of water and add salt. Parboil *shungiku* leaves for about 1 minute, then remove and rinse in cold water. Drain and squeeze gently to remove any excess water. Cut lengthwise into 4 equal portions.

Mix ingredients for dashi soy in a saucepan and bring to the boil.

Place boiled *shungiku* on individual serving plates and serve with dashi soy.

As the stems are usually tougher than the leaves, boil the stems first so the vegetable will have an even texture.

In *shojin* cooking, cooked vegetables remain fresh and appealing. This is because vegetables are lightly cooked and seasoned, and any tougher portions are cooked longer so the texture is even.

BAMBOO SHOOTS
with MISO

Serves 4

260 g (9¹/₄ oz) boiled
bamboo shoots (page 21)

0.5-cm (¹/₄-in) slice red chilli

1 tsp sesame oil

MISO DRESSING

1 Tbsp white miso

1 Tbsp sake

Prepare boiled bamboo shoots and slice crosswise
into chunks.

Cut red chilli in half and remove the seeds.

To make miso dressing, mix white miso with sake.
Set aside.

Heat sesame oil in a saucepan and add red chilli.
Fry briefly. Add bamboo shoots and fry until a little
charred around the edges. Turn off heat and add
miso dressing to coat bamboo shoots.

Arrange on individual serving plates and serve.

For a spicier dish, cook the red chilli with the seeds. If using
canned or vacuum-packed bamboo shoots, rinse with water
before adding to the pan.

There is no better way to celebrate the arrival of spring than by enjoying sweet and crunchy bamboo shoots. This delicacy is lightly seasoned with miso and has a touch of spiciness from the red chilli.

SPRING CROQUETTES

Serves 4

45 g (1¹/₂ oz) carrot

25 g (⁴/₅ oz) coriander
leaves (cilantro)

200 g (7 oz) potatoes

200 g (7 oz) sweet potatoes

100 g (3¹/₂ oz) black
sesame seeds, or as needed

Sea salt, as needed

Vegetable oil for
deep-frying

BATTER

120 g (4¹/₃ oz) plain
(all-purpose) flour

130 ml (4¹/₃ fl oz) water

Peel and dice carrot, then boil in water for 5 minutes.
Remove and drain well.

Chop coriander and set aside.

Peel and cut potatoes and sweet potatoes into chunks.
Boil in water for 15 minutes or until tender. Remove
and drain well.

Mash potatoes and sweet potatoes evenly. Season with
salt. Add boiled diced carrot and chopped coriander
and mix well. Divide into 8 equal portions and roll each
portion into a ball.

To make batter, mix together flour and water. Dip balls
in the batter and coat well with black sesame seeds.
Gently flatten balls into an oval shape.

Heat oil and deep-fry balls for about 1 minute. Remove
and drain on absorbent paper. Arrange 2 croquettes on
each serving plate and serve.

Potato croquettes are a favourite with many, but nothing beats a croquette made with a variety of spring vegetables. Instead of breadcrumbs, these croquettes are coated with fragrant black sesame seeds and there is the distinct aroma of coriander leaves when you bite into them.

BRAISED BURDOCK and CARROT

Serves 4

3 Tbsp konbu dashi (page 19)

40-cm (16-in) burdock (*gobo*)

100 g (3¹⁄₂ oz) carrot

2 Tbsp vegetable oil

3 Tbsp Japanese soy sauce

3 Tbsp mirin

1 Tbsp raw sugar

Prepare konbu dashi. Set aside.

Peel burdock and cut thin sticks about 5-cm (2-in) long. Soak in water immediately to avoid discolouration. Peel and cut carrot into similar sticks.

Heat oil in a frying pan. Add burdock and stir-fry for 5 minutes. Add carrot sticks and stir-fry for another 5 minutes.

Add konbu dashi, soy sauce, mirin and sugar. Simmer over low heat until liquid is reduced.

Arrange on individual serving plates and serve.

To ensure that the vegetables are evenly cooked, always start by cooking those that require a longer cooking time. For this dish, it would be the burdock.

Burdock is believed to have detoxifying properties
and is considered a health food. In this recipe,
it is paired with carrot for a simple yet nourishing dish.

SHISO RICE
Serves 4

Japanese rice (page 19)

2 green shiso leaves

Prepare Japanese rice.

Remove and discard stems of shiso leaves. Wash and pat dry, then chop leaves finely and add to rice. Mix well and serve.

Shiso leaves have a distinctive taste. The finer it is chopped, the more intensive the flavour.

CLEAR VEGETABLE BROTH
Serves 4

1.25 litres (40 fl oz / 5 cups) mushroom dashi (page 20)

80 g (2⁴/₅ oz) carrot

100 g (3¹/₂ oz) daikon

2.5-cm (1-in) knob ginger

2 Tbsp sesame oil

3 Tbsp Japanese soy sauce

¹/₂ tsp sea salt

Prepare mushroom dashi and set aside.

Peel carrot and daikon. Cut each root vegetable into 8 chunky pieces. Peel ginger and cut into 3 or 4 slices.

Heat sesame oil in a pot and add ginger slices. Fry for about 1 minute. Add carrot and daikon chunks and cook until a little charred around the edges.

Add mushroom dashi, soy sauce and salt and bring to the boil. Lower heat and simmer for 15-20 minutes, skimming off and discarding any foam that rises to the surface from time to time.

Serve hot.

CABBAGE ROLLS

Serves 4

750 ml (24 fl oz / 3 cups) mushroom dashi (page 20)

120 g (4¹/₃ oz) carrot

4 pieces *abura-age*

4 white cabbage leaves

3 Tbsp Japanese soy sauce

1 Tbsp sake

¹/₂ tsp sea salt

Prepare mushroom dashi and cut mushrooms into short, thin strips. Do the same with carrot and *abura-age*. Boil carrot until tender. Drain well.

Soften white cabbage leaves by boiling briefly. Drain and set aside to cool.

Lay a leaf on a chopping board with the underside facing up. Make shallow parallel cuts on the stem so the leaf can be rolled up easily. Turn the leaf over and top with some slices of mushroom, carrot and *abura-age*. Roll the leaf up. Secure with a toothpick. Repeat with the remaining ingredients.

Bring mushroom dashi to a boil. Add cabbage rolls, soy sauce, sake and salt and boil for 5–8 minutes.

Remove and arrange 2 cabbage rolls on each serving plate. Serve drizzled with mushroom dashi.

Vary this recipe by substituting the vegetables used.

If you are preparing the clear vegetable broth (page 42) for the meal as well, you may omit the mushroom dashi and simply boil the cabbage rolls in the vegetable broth. This will also add depth of flavour to the vegetable broth.

Handle the cabbage leaves gently to avoid tearing them.
Boiling the cabbage rolls in the dashi and serving
the dashi as the sauce is the *shojin* way of
making full use of each ingredient.

ASPARAGUS with WALNUT-MISO DRESSING

Serves 4

32 thin asparagus spears

WALNUT-MISO DRESSING

20 g (²/₃ oz) walnuts

2 tsp white miso

2 tsp mirin

1 tsp flaxseed oil

Prepare walnut-miso dressing. Heat a frying pan over medium heat and add walnuts. Stir constantly for 2-3 minutes until walnuts start to brown. Remove from heat immediately.

Grind toasted walnuts with a *suribachi* or mortar and pestle. Transfer ground walnuts to a bowl and add miso, mirin and flaxseed oil. Mix well and set aside.

Trim root ends of asparagus and blanch in boiling water. Drain and cool under running water and drain again. Cut asparagus into halves or thirds lengthwise. Coat with walnut-miso dressing.

Arrange on individual serving plates and serve.

Drain the asparagus well before mixing with the dressing or the dressing will not adhere to the asparagus spears.

This intense walnut-miso dressing
will lift any plain cooked vegetable.
Mirin is added to provide a touch of sweetness.

BAMBOO SHOOTS
with SESAME

Serves 4

260 g (9¼ oz) boiled bamboo shoots (page 21)

500 ml (16 fl oz / 2 cups) konbu dashi (page 19)

1 Tbsp Japanese soy sauce

2 Tbsp sake

⅓ tsp sea salt

3 Tbsp toasted and ground sesame seeds (page 21)

Prepare boiled bamboo shoots and cut into bite-size wedges. Set aside.

Prepare konbu dashi and bring to the boil with soy sauce, sake and salt. Lower heat, add boiled bamboo shoots and simmer for 30 minutes.

Prepare toasted and ground sesame seeds.

Divide bamboo shoots equally among 4 serving bowls. Top with some toasted and ground sesame seeds and stock. Serve.

Lift the flavour of this dish by topping it with some finely grated yuzu rind or lemon rind.

This dish allows you to enjoy bamboo shoot
in its purest form. The bamboo shoot remains sweet
and crisp, with a subtle savoury flavour from the
konbu dashi in which it is simmered.

GANMODOKI (Tofu Fritters)

Serves 4

320 g (11¼ oz) silken tofu

4 g (⅛ oz) dried *hijiki* seaweed

60 g (2¼ oz) carrot

150 g (5⅓ oz) *yamatoimo*

36 g (1⅕ oz) corn kernels

70 g (2½ oz) *katakuniku* or potato starch

Vegetable oil for deep-frying

SAUCE

200 ml (6¾ fl oz) mushroom dashi (page 20)

50 ml (1⅔ fl oz) Japanese soy sauce

50 ml (1⅔ fl oz) mirin

Wrap silken tofu with paper towels and place on a plate. Place another plate on top of tofu to act as a weight and refrigerate for 30 minutes. This is to remove excess water from the tofu.

Wash *hijiki* seaweed and soak in water for 20 minutes. Remove and drain well.

To make sauce, prepare mushroom dashi and bring to the boil with soy sauce and mirin. Set aside to cool.

Peel and dice carrot. Peel *yamatoimo* and remove any black spots. Finely grate.

Remove tofu from the refrigerator. Peel off paper towels and transfer tofu to a bowl. Mash finely. Add grated *yamatoimo*, carrot, *hijiki*, corn and *katakuniku* or potato starch and mix thoroughly. Divide into 8 equal portions and shape into patties.

Heat oil and deep-fry tofu patties until golden brown. Serve with sauce.

Wet your palms before shaping the tofu mixture to keep the mixture from sticking to your hands.

These tofu fritters are the meatballs of *shojin ryori*. Ready-made *ganmodoki* is available from Japanese supermarkets, but nothing beats the soft and melting texture of a freshly-made *ganmodoki*.

VINEGARED CARROT

Serves 4

150 g (5⅓ oz) carrot

1 tsp sea salt

2 Tbsp toasted white
sesame seeds

VINAIGRETTE DRESSING

4 Tbsp rice vinegar

2 Tbsp Japanese soy sauce

2 Tbsp mirin

1 tsp raw sugar

Peel and julienne carrot. In a mixing bowl, toss carrot
with salt and let stand for 20 minutes. Rinse carrot and
drain well.

Combine all ingredients for dressing in a bowl and
mix well. Add carrot and set aside to marinate for
2-3 hours.

Place vinegared carrot into individual serving bowls.
Sprinkle with sesame seeds and serve.

....

This dish can be prepared a day ahead and kept
refrigerated until ready to serve.

This vinaigrette dressing is also known as *san bai zu*. It is one of the essential sauces in Japanese cooking. Here, it dresses a simple salad and sesame seeds add fragrance and a nutty flavour.

The weather turns warm and you know summer
has arrived. Vegetables in various hues and colours
appear in the markets. In the summer menu that follows,
you will find dishes brightened by these
colourful summer vegetables.

夏 Summer

VEGETABLE SUSHI RICE

Serves 4

Japanese rice (page 19)

5-cm (2-in) length lotus root

1 Tbsp rice vinegar

40 g (1¹/₃ oz) carrot

30 g (1 oz) sugar snap peas

SUSHI DRESSING

4 Tbsp rice vinegar

3 tsp sea salt

6 Tbsp raw sugar

VINEGAR MIXTURE

2 Tbsp raw sugar

4 Tbsp rice vinegar

Prepare Japanese rice.

Prepare sushi dressing. Combine vinegar, salt and sugar in a pot. Place over low heat and stir until sugar and salt are dissolved. Remove from heat and set aside to cool.

Peel and slice lotus root into thin rings. Boil a pot of water and add 1 Tbsp vinegar. Add sliced lotus root and boil for 5 minutes. Drain well.

Prepare vinegar mixture. Dissolve sugar in vinegar. Add boiled sliced lotus root and let soak for 30 minutes.

Peel and dice carrot. Boil a pot of water and add carrot. Cook until tender. Remove and drain well.

Trim and string sugar snap peas. Boil a pot of water and cook sugar snap peas for 2 minutes. Remove and drain well. Cut into thin slices.

Transfer cooked rice to a big bowl. Toss rice and let it cool for a few minutes. Gradually add sushi dressing and use a rice spatula to fold rice from the bottom to the top. Add carrot and sugar snap peas and mix well.

Spoon sushi rice into serving bowls. Top with slices of lotus root and serve.

Use gentle strokes as you fold the rice, so it does not become mushy.

While mixing the rice with the dressing, use a fan to cool the rice. This will give the rice an appetising shiny texture.

MISO SOUP with SILKEN TOFU

Serves 4

Konbu dashi (page 19)

320 g (11¼ oz) silken tofu

4 Tbsp white miso

Prepare konbu dashi and while it is simmering, crush silken tofu into coarse pieces and add to the pot.

Pass miso through a fine sieve into the stock and stir until dissolved.

Spoon soup and tofu into serving bowls and serve.

Passing the miso through the sieve will prevent any residue in the miso getting into the soup. Once the miso has been added, do not boil the soup or the beneficial properties of the miso will be destroyed.

In *shojin* cooking, tofu is not cut into delicate cubes and added to soup, but crumbled into pieces. This is the Zen belief of equanimity. This way, everyone, regardless of status, would get a fair share of the tofu.

Vegetable Sushi Rice

Miso Soup with Silken Tofu

In Japanese cuisine, rice and
miso soup are like husband and wife.
They are almost always served together.

MASHED PUMPKIN with WATER CHESTNUT

Serves 4

400 ml (13 fl oz) konbu dashi (page 19)

1 tsp Japanese soy sauce

1 tsp + 1 Tbsp raw sugar

300 g (11 oz) Japanese pumpkin

200 g (7 oz) potatoes

4 water chestnuts

30 g (1 oz) raisins

4 tsp unsweetened soy milk

Prepare konbu dashi and bring to the boil. Add soy sauce and 1 tsp sugar.

Peel and cut pumpkin and potatoes into chunks. Add to the konbu dashi and boil for 20 minutes or until tender. Transfer to a colander and drain well.

Peel water chestnuts and dice.

Place a pan over low heat. Add boiled pumpkin and potato chunks and mash in the pan. This will help remove excess liquid from the mash. Add diced water chestnuts, raisins, soy milk and remaining 1 Tbsp sugar. Mix well.

Spoon into individual serving plates and serve.

For a firmer texture, refrigerate the pumpkin mash for 2 hours before serving.

The water chestnuts add crunch to the mash and should not be diced too finely.

This smooth and creamy mashed pumpkin is my alternative to ice cream. This is certainly a delight in the summer especially with the addition of plump, juicy raisins and crunchy water chestnuts which add textural interest to the mash.

EGGPLANT with GOMA DRESSING

Serves 4

4 Japanese eggplants (*nasu*), each about 70 g (2½ oz)

Vegetable oil for deep-frying

GOMA DRESSING

3 Tbsp toasted and ground sesame seeds (page 21)

3 Tbsp Japanese soy sauce

1½ Tbsp sake

1½ Tbsp raw sugar

Wash and trim ends of eggplants. Cut each eggplant into halves lengthwise and pat dry.

Prepare toasted and ground sesame seeds for *goma* dressing and mix with soy sauce, sake and sugar until sugar is dissolved.

Heat oil and slide eggplant pieces gently into hot oil, skin side down. Deep-fry for about 1 minute, then turn pieces over and deep-fry other side until brown. Remove and drain on absorbent paper.

Arrange 2 slices of eggplant on each serving dish. Top with *goma* dressing and serve.

You can use other varieties of eggplant when making this dish, but the Japanese eggplant is most suitable as it has a delicate flavour, thin skin and few seeds.

If preferred, the eggplant can also be grilled rather than deep-fried.

This dish is a must for all eggplant lovers!
I always get special requests to prepare it when catering
for private functions. The juicy eggplant pairs perfectly
with the *goma* dressing.

BROCCOLI with TOMATO

Serves 4

300 g (11 oz) broccoli

1 tsp sea salt

TOMATO SAUCE

1 medium tomato, about 100 g (3$^1/_2$ oz)

2 Tbsp olive oil

1 Tbsp rice vinegar

1 Tbsp Japanese soy sauce

$^1/_4$ tsp sea salt

1 tsp raw sugar

Prepare tomato sauce. Cut tomato in half and remove and discard soft centre. Dice tomato and mix with olive oil, vinegar, soy sauce, salt and sugar. Set aside.

Trim broccoli to bite-size pieces. Boil a pot of water and add salt. Add broccoli stems and cook for 2 minutes. Add broccoli florets and boil for another 3 minutes. Remove and plunge into cold water to stop the cooking process. This will help the broccoli retain its fresh green colour and crunchy texture. Drain well.

Arrange broccoli on individual serving plates. Top with tomato sauce and serve.

Do not overcook the broccoli or it will lose its taste and texture. Overcooked broccoli will also break apart easily. The stems take a longer time to cook, so put them into the pot to cook first.

Broccoli is one of nature's wonder foods.
In this recipe, it is lightly cooked,
then topped with a refreshing tomato dressing.
Serve it arranged in small bowls.

PAN-FRIED
SPICY CUCUMBER

Serves 4

2 Japanese cucumbers,
each about 90 g (3¼ oz)

Sea salt, as needed

3-cm (1¼-in) slice red chilli

4 Tbsp sesame oil

2 Tbsp Japanese soy sauce

1 Tbsp sake

1 tsp rice vinegar

Shichimi togarashi, to taste

Rub cucumbers with salt.

Place a cucumber between a pair of chopsticks and cut thinly at a diagonal without cutting through. (The chopsticks will help ensure that you do not cut all the way through.) Turn the cucumber over and repeat to cut thinly at a diagonal without cutting through. Repeat for the other cucumber.

Using your hands, break each cucumber into 4 or 5 pieces.

Cut red chilli in half and remove the seeds.

Heat sesame oil in a saucepan and fry chilli briefly. Lower heat and add soy sauce, sake, vinegar and *shichimi togarashi*. Mix well.

Add cucumber and cook briefly for 30–60 seconds.

Arrange on individual serving plates and serve.

Cook the cucumbers lightly to retain their crunchiness.

 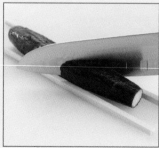 

When I first learnt to prepare this dish,
I was intrigued by the cutting technique.
The cucumber stays in one piece and the cuts help
the cucumber absorb the seasoning.
This refreshing dish will be a delight to those
who like their food spicy.

SOY MILK JELLY with TOMATO and EDAMAME

Serves 4

100 ml (3¹/₂ fl oz) konbu dashi (page 19)

A pinch of sea salt

40 g (1¹/₃ oz) edamame

40 g (1¹/₃ oz) tomato

3 g (¹/₁₀ oz) *kanten* powder

100 ml (3¹/₂ fl oz) unsweetened soy milk

SAUCE

100 ml (3¹/₂ fl oz) konbu dashi (page 19)

1 Tbsp Japanese soy sauce

1 Tbsp raw sugar

1 Tbsp cornflour

Prepare konbu dashi and measure out portions needed for jelly and sauce. Set aside.

Boil a pot of water and add salt. Add edamame and boil for 5 minutes. Remove, drain and set aside to cool. Squeeze beans out from the pods using your fingers and remove thin membranes.

Slice tomato in half. Remove and discard soft centre. Dice tomato.

Mix *kanten* powder with some soy milk to form a runny paste.

Heat konbu dashi and remaining soy milk in a pan over medium heat. Add *kanten* paste and stir well. When mixture starts to boil, turn off heat.

Spread edmame and diced tomato evenly in a 17.5 x 8 x 6-cm (7 x 3 x 2¹/₃-in) metal tray. Pour konbu-soymilk mixture over and let it cool to room temperature. Refrigerate for about 30 minutes or until jelly is set.

To make sauce, combine 100 ml (3¹/₂ fl oz) konbu dashi, soy sauce and sugar in a pot. Bring to a boil over medium heat. Lower heat to a simmer. Mix cornflour with just enough water to get a slurry, then whisk it into simmering mixture to thicken it.

Turn set jelly from tray onto a cutting board and cut into 4 pieces. Arrange on individual serving plates. Garnish as desired and top with thickened sauce. Serve.

....

Removing the thin membrane from the edamame gives the beans a glossy appearance.

Kanten is a natural vegetable gelatin that contains no calories and is high in dietary fibre. Dotted with tomato and edamame, this soy milk jelly resembles jewels. A guest once described it as a piece of white jade with subtle shades of red and green.

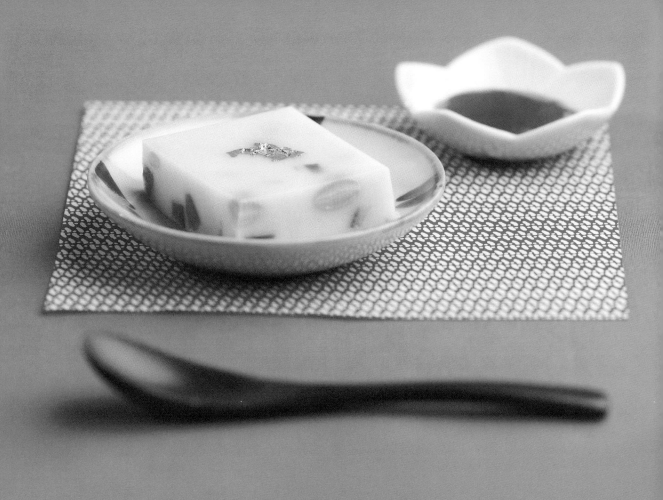

VEGETABLE SUSHI RICE

Serves 4

Japanese rice (page 19)

5-cm (2-in) length lotus root

1 Tbsp rice vinegar

40 g (1 1/3 oz) carrot

30 g (1 oz) sugar snap peas

SUSHI DRESSING

4 Tbsp rice vinegar

3 tsp sea salt

6 Tbsp raw sugar

VINEGAR MIXTURE

2 Tbsp raw sugar

4 Tbsp rice vinegar

Prepare Japanese rice.

Prepare sushi dressing. Combine vinegar, salt and sugar in a pot. Place over low heat and stir until sugar and salt are dissolved. Remove from heat and set aside to cool.

Peel and slice lotus root into thin rings. Boil a pot of water and add 1 Tbsp vinegar. Add sliced lotus root and boil for 5 minutes. Drain well.

Prepare vinegar mixture. Dissolve sugar in vinegar. Add boiled sliced lotus root and let soak for 30 minutes.

Peel and dice carrot. Boil a pot of water and add carrot. Cook until tender. Remove and drain well.

Trim and string sugar snap peas. Boil a pot of water and cook sugar snap peas for 2 minutes. Remove and drain well. Cut into thin slices.

Transfer cooked rice to a big bowl. Toss rice and let it cool for a few minutes. Gradually add sushi dressing and use a rice spatula to fold rice from the bottom to the top. Add carrot and sugar snap peas and mix well.

Spoon sushi rice into serving bowls. Top with slices of lotus root and serve.

Use gentle strokes as you fold the rice, so it does not become mushy.

While mixing the rice with the dressing, use a fan to cool the rice. This will give the rice an appetising shiny texture.

MISO SOUP with SILKEN TOFU

Serves 4

Konbu dashi (page 19)

320 g (11¼ oz) silken tofu

4 Tbsp white miso

Prepare konbu dashi and while it is simmering, crush silken tofu into coarse pieces and add to the pot.

Pass miso through a fine sieve into the stock and stir until dissolved.

Spoon soup and tofu into serving bowls and serve.

Passing the miso through the sieve will prevent any residue in the miso getting into the soup. Once the miso has been added, do not boil the soup or the beneficial properties of the miso will be destroyed.

In *shojin* cooking, tofu is not cut into delicate cubes and added to soup, but crumbled into pieces. This is the Zen belief of equanimity. This way, everyone, regardless of status, would get a fair share of the tofu.

Vegetable Sushi Rice

Miso Soup with Silken Tofu

The colours of summer are reflected in this dish of plain sushi rice mixed with brightly coloured vegetables.

STEWED PUMPKIN

Serves 4

400 g (14^1/$_3$ oz) Japanese pumpkin

500 ml (16 fl oz / 2 cups) water

6 Tbsp raw sugar

1 tsp sea salt

If the skin of the pumpkin is tough, use a vegetable peeler to shave off the skin. If the skin is tender, the pumpkin can be eaten with the skin. Cut the pumpkin into wedges.

Heat water, sugar and salt in a saucepan over medium heat. Stir to dissolve sugar and salt. Bring to the boil and add pumpkin wedges. Lower heat and simmer for about 20 minutes or until pumpkin is tender.

Remove pumpkin wedges and arrange on individual serving plates. Spoon a little of the simmering liquid over and serve.

If it is not too tough, the skin of the Japanese pumpkin is edible and does not need to be shaved off. The skin will also add colour to the dish.

Watch the pumpkin as it simmers so it does not become too soft, making it hard to handle.

The vibrant orange hue of the pumpkin will brighten any table. I usually add a subtle contrast of colour by leaving some of the green skin on.

SWEET POTATO with CUCUMBER PURÉE

Serves 4

2 Japanese cucumbers, each about 90 g (3¹/₄ oz)

4 Tbsp rice vinegar

2 Tbsp raw sugar

280 g (10 oz) Japanese sweet potatoes

Vegetable oil for deep-frying

Trim ends of cucumbers. Finely grate and place in a fine sieve to drain. Let excess liquid drip off. Do not press grated cucumber. Transfer to a bowl.

Add rice vinegar and sugar to grated cucumber and mix well. Set aside.

Wash and scrub sweet potatoes. Do not peel skin. Cut into bite-size pieces.

Heat oil and deep-fry sweet potatoes until golden brown. Remove and drain well.

Mix deep-fried sweet potatoes with grated cucumber and arrange on individual serving plates. Serve.

Keep the sweet potato pieces chunky so they will be soft inside and crisp outside after deep-frying.

The sweet-sour cucumber purée heightens the taste of the crisp sweet potato. This pairing works so well, it has intrigued many diners. Coat the sweet potato evenly with the purée to get the best out of the dish.

SIMMERED LADIES' FINGERS

Serves 4

180 g (6⅓ oz) ladies'
fingers (okra), or about
16 medium pieces

450 ml (15 fl oz) water

5 Tbsp Japanese soy sauce

4 Tbsp sake

2 Tbsp raw sugar

Wash and trim stem ends of ladies' fingers.

Place water, soy sauce, sake and sugar in a saucepan
and bring to the boil. Lower heat and add ladies'
fingers. Simmer for about 10 minutes.

Remove and cut each ladies' finger in half. Arrange on
individual serving plates.

Drizzle 1–2 Tbsp of the simmering liquid over ladies'
fingers and serve.

When selecting ladies' fingers, choose those that are evenly
green and firm in texture.

I did not like eating ladies' fingers until I learned
this simple recipe. It is amazing how *shojin ryori*
changed my perception of ladies fingers,
as I finally got the true taste of this vegetable.

CARROT CROQUETTES

Serves 4

320 g (11¼ oz) *momen* tofu

300 g (11 oz) carrots

½ tsp sea salt

40 g (1⅓ oz) chopped roasted peanuts

2 Tbsp cornflour

Plain (all-purpose) flour, for dusting

120 g (4⅓ oz) breadcrumbs

Vegetable oil for deep-frying

4 lemon wedges

BATTER

120 g (4⅓ oz) plain (all-purpose) flour

130 ml (4⅓ fl oz) water

Wrap *momen* tofu with paper towels and place on a plate. Place another plate on top of tofu to act as a weight and refrigerate for 30 minutes. This is to remove excess water from the tofu.

Peel and cut carrots into chunks. Boil a pot of water and cook carrots for 20 minutes or until tender. Transfer to a colander and drain well.

Remove tofu from the refrigerator. Peel off paper towels and set aside.

Heat a pan over low heat. Mash carrots in the pan. This is to remove excess liquid from the carrots. Turn off heat and add *momen* tofu. Mash tofu and add salt, peanuts and cornflour. Mix well.

Divide mixture into 8 portions and shape into oval patties. Dust patties with some flour.

Make a batter with the flour and water. Coat carrot patties with batter, then cover with breadcrumbs.

Heat oil and deep-fry patties for about 1 minute or until light brown. Remove and drain well on absorbent paper.

Arrange on individual serving plates with a wedge of lemon. Serve.

Substitute the peanuts with any of your favourite nuts.

Wet your hands when shaping the patties to keep the mixture from sticking to your hands.

Like the spring croquettes (page 36), these carrot croquettes are made with tofu, which gives them a light and refreshing texture. Adding peanuts gives the croquettes additional bite and flavour.

COURGETTE WRAP

Serves 4

1 yellow and 1 green
courgette (zucchini), each
about 300 g (11 oz)

Sea salt, as needed

100 g (3½ oz) tomato

1 Tbsp olive oil

1 tsp Japanese soy sauce

1 Tbsp sake

1 Tbsp white miso

Using a vegetable peeler, slice yellow and green
courgettes lengthwise into thin strips. Make 8 yellow
strips and 8 green strips.

Boil a pot of water and add a pinch of salt. Blanch
courgette strips for about 20 seconds. Drain well and
set aside to cool.

Cut tomato in half and remove and discard soft centre.
Dice tomato.

Remove and discard soft centres of remaining
courgettes and measure out 60 g (2¼ oz) of each
courgette. Use remaining courgette in another recipe.

Heat olive oil in a saucepan over low heat. Add diced
tomato and courgettes, a little salt, soy sauce, sake and
miso. Stir-fry for about 1 minute. Remove and set aside.

Line a small square mould with 2 courgette strips
(1 yellow and 1 green), leaving ends hanging over
mould. Place another 2 courgette strips (1 yellow and
1 green) perpendicularly over the first two, leaving
the ends hanging over the mould. Fill lined mould
with some tomato-courgette mixture. Fold ends of
courgette strips over filling and press lightly to ensure
it is firmly packed. Turn courgette wrap out of mould
onto a serving plate.

Repeat with remaining ingredients. Serve.

If the tomato-courgette mixture is too watery, place it into a
fine sieve to drain before wrapping.

The inspiration for this dish is from the *furoshiki,* the traditional wrapping cloth the Japnese use for carrying items. It is visually appealing and will have your guests anticipating what the parcel contains.

Autumn acts as a mediator between summer and winter. During this time, nature is coloured with different shades of red and yellow. It is also during this time that I fall in love with *momiji* (Japanese red maple leaves) all over again.

秋

Autumn

UDON NOODLES
with SESAME

Serves 4

4 Tbsp toasted and ground sesame seeds (page 21)

60 g (2¼ oz) daikon

2 bundles dried udon noodles

A handful of shredded seaweed

UDON SAUCE

100 ml (3½ fl oz) konbu dashi (page 19)

2 Tbsp Japanese soy sauce

2 Tbsp mirin

Prepare konbu dashi and toasted and ground sesame seeds. Set aside.

Peel and grate daikon finely. Place in a fine sieve to drain, then measure out 1 Tbsp grated daikon.

To prepare udon sauce, mix konbu dashi, soy sauce and mirin in a pot and bring to the boil. Set aside.

Boil a pot of water and add udon. Boil and stir for 6 minutes or according to instructions on pack until noodles are al dente. Drain and rinse under cold running water.

Divide udon equally among 4 serving bowls. Top with toasted and ground sesame seeds, grated daikon and shredded seaweed. Serve udon with a small cup of udon sauce. Pour sauce over udon and mix before eating.

Use a large pot of water when boiling the udon to prevent the noodles from getting starchy. To get a firm texture, rinse the noodles under cold running water immediately after draining.

MISO SOUP with NAMEKO MUSHROOMS

Serves 4

1.25 litres (40 fl oz / 5 cups) konbu dashi (page 19)

80 g (2⁴/₅ oz) *nameko* mushrooms

3 Tbsp white miso

1 Tbsp red miso

Briefly wash mushrooms and separate them.

Prepare konbu dashi. While konbu dashi is simmering, add mushrooms and cook for 1 minute. Remove and set aside.

Stir white and red miso through a fine sieve into konbu dashi until dissolved.

Spoon miso soup with mushrooms into individual serving bowls and serve.

. . . .

If using fresh *nameko* mushrooms, select those with shiny caps and a firm texture. If using canned or vacuum-packed *nameko* mushrooms, rinse briefly before cooking.

YAMATOIMO NORI NUGGETS

Serves 4

150 g (5¹/₃ oz) *yamatoimo*

1¹/₂ sheets nori (seaweed)

Vegetable oil for deep-frying

SAUCE

2.5-cm (1-in) knob ginger

2 tsp Japanese soy sauce

Prepare sauce. Peel and finely grate ginger, then squeeze to obtain 1 tsp ginger juice. Mix ginger juice and soy sauce. Set aside.

Peel *yamatoimo* and remove any black spots. Finely grate. Divide into 12 equal portions.

Cut nori into 12 equal pieces. (Cut the full sheet into eighths and the half-sheet into quarters.)

Place a portion of grated *yamatoimo* at one end of each nori piece. Roll up.

Heat the vegetable oil over medium heat. Slide the rolls into the hot oil and deep-fry for 1–2 minutes untll light brown. Remove and drain.

Coat the nuggets with sauce and arrange on individual serving plates. Serve hot.

....

When making these nuggets, do not roll them too tightly as the *yamatoimo* will expand upon frying and may overflow at both ends if the roll is too tight.

Grated *yamatoimo* wrapped with nori
and deep-fried is reminiscent of Japanese fishcake.
The spongy texture of these nuggets
goes well with the ginger sauce.

NAGAIMO MUSHROOM CROQUETTES

Serves 4

200 g (7 oz) *nagaimo*

3 tsp white miso

120 g (4^1/$_3$ oz) breadcrumbs

8 large shiitake mushrooms

Plain (all-purpose) flour, for dusting

Vegetable oil for deep-frying

4 lemon wedges

BATTER

120 g (4^1/$_3$ oz) plain (all-purpose) flour

130 ml (4^1/$_3$ fl oz) water

Peel *nagaimo* and remove any black spots. Cut into chunks. Boil a pot of water and add *nagaimo*. Boil for 15 minutes or until tender. Remove and drain well.

Heat a pan over low heat. Mash *nagaimo* in the pan. This is to remove excess liquid from the nagaimo. Add miso and half the breadcrumbs. Mix well.

Wipe mushroom caps and cut off stems. Fill underside of a mushroom cap with *nagaimo* mixture and smoothen with a spoon or knife. Sandwich with another mushroom cap. Repeat with remaining mushrooms and *nagaimo* mixture.

Dust mushroom croquettes with flour.

Make a batter with flour and water. Coat mushroom croquettes with batter, then breadcrumbs.

Heat oil and deep-fry croquettes for about 1 minute or until light golden brown. Remove and drain on absorbent paper.

Arrange on individual serving plates and serve with lemon wedges on the side.

Replace *nagaimo* with other varieties of mountain yam if *nagaimo* is unavailable.

Serve these golden croquettes freshly deep-fried
to enjoy the combination of shiitake mushrooms
and *nagaimo*—two layers of softness—
that simply melts in your mouth.

HIJIKI TERIYAKI

Serves 4

10 g (¹/₃ oz) dried *hijiki*

40 g (1¹/₃ oz) carrot

1 Tbsp sesame oil

3 Tbsp Japanese soy sauce

3 Tbsp mirin

2 Tbsp raw sugar

Soak dried *hijiki* in water for about 20 minutes. Drain well.

Peel carrot and julienne.

Heat sesame oil in a pan. Add carrot sticks and stir-fry for 2 minutes. Add *hijiki* and stir-fry for 1 minute. Add soy sauce, mirin and sugar and cook for another minute.

Arrange on individual serving plates and serve.

Carrot is typically included to add colour to this dish. It can be substituted with other vegetables such as green beans.

The Japanese believe that regular consumption
of *hijiki* is the secret behind their thick, lustrous hair.
If you intend to share this information with your guests,
be prepared to offer second helpings of this dish!

YURINE CITRUS BALLS

Serves 4

2-4 fresh yurine (lily bulbs)

1 orange, rind only

2 Tbsp sake

3 Tbsp raw sugar

3 Tbsp water

Wash yurine bulbs and trim the base. You will end up with many petals. Carefully remove any black spots. Steam yurine petals until soft and translucent. Set aside to cool.

Press steamed yurine petals through a fine sieve into a smooth paste. Divide the yurine paste into 8 portions. Set aside.

Use a zester, cut fine short strips from orange rind.

Place sake, sugar and water in a saucepan and bring to the boil over medium heat, stirring to dissolve sugar. Lower heat and add grated orange rind. Simmer for 1 minute or until rind is tender and has absorbed some of the solution. Set aside to cool.

Place a portion of yurine paste in your palm and add a few strips of orange rind. Roll into a ball. Repeat with the remaining ingredients.

Arrange on individual serving plates and serve.

Vary the flavour of these citrus balls by using other citrus fruits such as lemon, lime or mandarin oranges.

I enjoy preparing this dish, as the sweet perfume of the yurine bulbs fill the kitchen when they are steamed. In Japanese cooking, ingredients are often pushed through a fine mesh sieve to obtain a smooth paste. This is a simple yet elegant dish that can also be served as a snack.

SPINACH and MUSHROOM with CITRUS DRESSING

Serves 4

4 medium dried shiitake mushrooms

1 tsp vegetable oil

250 g (9 oz) spinach

$^1/_2$ tsp sea salt

CITRUS DRESSING

4 Tbsp Japanese soy sauce

1 Tbsp lemon juice

Rinse dried shiitake mushrooms and reconstitute by soaking in a bowl of water for about 3 hours or simmering in a pot of water for 10–15 minutes.

Squeeze excess water from mushrooms, then julienne. Heat oil in a pan and pan-fry mushrooms for about 3 minutes. Remove and set aside.

Trim off crowns or stem clusters of spinach leaves. (Reserve crowns or stem clusters and prepare as an additional dish if preferred. See note below.) Rinse spinach leaves well.

Boil a pot of water and add salt. Parboil spinach leaves for about 1 minute, then remove and rinse in cold water. Drain and squeeze gently to remove any excess water. Cut lengthwise into 4 equal portions.

Mix soy sauce and lemon juice for the citrus dressing.

Arrange mushroom and spinach on individual serving plates. Top with citrus dressing and serve.

As the stems are usually tougher than the leaves, boil the stems first, followed by the leaves. This will give the spinach an even texture.

The spinach crowns can be prepared as a side dish. Simply braise with some salt and sake for about 2 minutes.

This is a delight for those who like the refreshing sour taste of lemon. The citrus dressing, made with a combination of soy sauce and lemon juice adds tang to this simple dish of spinach and mushrooms.

UDON NOODLES with SESAME

Serves 4

4 Tbsp toasted and ground sesame seeds (page 21)

60 g (2¼ oz) daikon

2 bundles dried udon noodles

A handful of shredded seaweed

UDON SAUCE

100 ml (3½ fl oz) konbu dashi (page 19)

2 Tbsp Japanese soy sauce

2 Tbsp mirin

Prepare konbu dashi and toasted and ground sesame seeds. Set aside.

Peel and grate daikon finely. Place in a fine sieve to drain, then measure out 1 Tbsp grated daikon.

To prepare udon sauce, mix konbu dashi, soy sauce and mirin in a pot and bring to the boil. Set aside.

Boil a pot of water and add udon. Boil and stir for 6 minutes or according to instructions on pack until noodles are al dente. Drain and rinse under cold running water.

Divide udon equally among 4 serving bowls. Top with toasted and ground sesame seeds, grated daikon and shredded seaweed. Serve udon with a small cup of udon sauce. Pour sauce over udon and mix before eating.

Use a large pot of water when boiling the udon to prevent the noodles from getting starchy. To get a firm texture, rinse the noodles under cold running water immediately after draining.

Note: The udon noodles with sesame and miso soup with nameko mushrooms recipes have been reproduced from pages 88 and 89 for completeness and easy reference.

MISO SOUP with NAMEKO MUSHROOMS

Serves 4

1.25 litres (40 fl oz / 5 cups) konbu dashi (page 19)

80 g (2⁴/₅ oz) *nameko* mushrooms

3 Tbsp white miso

1 Tbsp red miso

Briefly wash mushrooms and separate them.

Prepare konbu dashi. While konbu dashi is simmering, add mushrooms and cook for 1 minute. Remove and set aside.

Stir white and red miso through a fine sieve into konbu dashi until dissolved.

Spoon miso soup with mushrooms into individual serving bowls and serve.

....

If using fresh *nameko* mushrooms, select those with shiny caps and a firm texture. If using canned or vacuum-packed *nameko* mushrooms, rinse briefly before cooking.

VEGETABLE TEMPURA

Serves 4

400 g (14$^1/_3$ oz) sweet potatoes

1 large firm persimmon

4 medium shiitake mushrooms

Plain (all-purpose) flour, for dusting

Vegetable oil for deep-frying

TEMPURA BATTER

120 g (4$^1/_3$ oz) plain (all-purpose) flour

130 ml (4$^1/_3$ fl oz) water

Sea salt, as needed

Wash and scrub the sweet potatoes. Cut into round slices. Remove the calyx from the persimmon and rinse. Cut into eighths. Wipe the mushrooms and cut into halves with the stems intact.

Combine the ingredients for the tempura batter and mix well.

Dust the sweet potatoes, persimmon and mushrooms with flour, then coat with tempura batter just before deep-frying.

Heat oil and deep-fry coated ingredients for about 1 minute or until light brown. Do this in batches. Remove and drain on absorbent paper.

Arrange on individual serving plates and serve immediately.

....

As tempura is best served hot, prepare this dish just before serving.

The Zen philosophy of minimising wastage extends to
dishware too. Tempura is often served with an extra bowl
of sauce for dipping, but in *shojin ryori,* the sauce
is done away with by adding a little salt to the batter.
The persimmon tempura never fails to delight
and surprise. Try it for yourself!

NAGAIMO
CHANWAN MUSHI

Serves 4

3 Tbsp mushroom dashi
(page 20)

2 tsp vegetable oil

2 tsp raw sugar

2 tsp Japanese soy sauce

2 tsp sake

12 gingko nuts

200 g (7 oz) *nagaimo*

CHAWAN MUSHI SAUCE

100 ml (3¹/₂ fl oz)
mushroom dashi (page 20)

2 tsp raw sugar

2 tsp Japanese soy sauce

2 tsp potato starch

Prepare mushroom dashi. Reserve 3 mushrooms
and dice.

Heat oil and stir-fry diced mushrooms briefly. Add
3 Tbsp mushroom dashi, sugar, soy sauce and sake.
Stir-fry for about 3 minutes. Set aside.

Shell ginkgo nuts and soak in hot water to loosen skin.
Peel and discard skin, then boil until nuts are a delicate
shade of green. Set aside.

Peel *nagaimo* and remove any black spots. Grate finely.

Divide grated *nagaimo*, ginkgo nuts and mushrooms
equally among 4 individual *chawan mushi* cups. Cover
with aluminium foil and steam for about 5 minutes.

Prepare *chawan mushi* sauce. Heat mushroom dashi,
sugar and soy sauce in a saucepan over medium heat.
Bring to the boil, then lower heat to a simmer.
Mix potato starch with a little water to get a slurry.
Add to simmering sauce and whisk until thickened.

Spoon some *chawan mushi* sauce into each cup
and serve hot.

To thicken the *chawan mushi* sauce, cornflour or *kuzu* can
also be used.

Chawan mushi literally means steaming in a tea cup and it is commonly known to be a steamed egg custard. Adopting a similar method of steaming, I have replaced the eggs with grated *nagaimo* which turns smooth and starchy upon steaming.

VEGETABLE OKARA (SOY PULP)

Serves 4

15 g (¹/₂ oz) carrot

15 g (¹/₂ oz) burdock (*gobo*)

3 sweet beans

1 Tbsp sesame oil

200 g (7 oz) *okara* (soy pulp)

SEASONING

250 ml (8 fl oz / 1 cup) mushroom dashi (page 20)

2 Tbsp Japanese soy sauce

2 Tbsp mirin

1 Tbsp raw sugar

Prepare mushroom dashi. Reserve 2 mushrooms.

Peel and julienne carrot and burdock. Soak burdock immediately in water to avoid discolouration. Drain before using. Julienne mushrooms and sweet beans.

Heat sesame oil and stir-fry burdock for 3 minutes. Add carrot and mushrooms and cook for 2 minutes. Add sweet beans and *okara* and cook for another minute. Season with mushroom dashi, soy sauce, mirin and sugar and stir-fry for 3 minutes.

Arrange on individual serving plates and serve.

....

If preferred, add a little more dashi when stir-frying so the final dish is more moist.

Okara is a by-product of tofu and soy milk making, and it is often discarded. Though high in protein, *okara* is bland and needs to be cooked with other ingredients and seasoned for flavour.

YAMATOIMO NORI ROLLS

Serves 4

250 g (9 oz) *yamatoimo*

2 Tbsp raw sugar

¹/₂ tsp sea salt

1 sheet nori (seaweed)

1 Tbsp wasabi

Peel *yamatoimo* and remove any black spots. Cut into chunks.

Boil a pot of water and add *yamatoimo*. Boil for 15 minutes or until tender. Remove and drain well.

Heat a pan over low heat. Mash *yamatoimo* in the pan. This is to remove excess liquid from the *yamatoimo*. Add sugar and salt. Mix well.

Place nori sheet on a sushi mat and spread mashed *yamatoimo* evenly over nori, leaving a small border along the edges. Make an indent on the *yamatoimo* layer along one length and spread with wasabi.

Roll up nori, then firmly squeeze to shape into a solid round roll. Cut into 12 equal pieces and arrange on individual serving plates. Serve.

When making the roll, have the glossy surface of the nori sheet facing down, so the rolls will have a glossy finish.

Store excess nori sheets in an airtight container in cool, dry place.

These may look like ordinary sushi rice rolls,
but these nori rolls are filled with sweet *yamatoimo* mash.
With their light and elegant texture, these nori rolls
will be a welcome alternative to heavier rice rolls.

GREEN BEANS with WALNUT-MISO DRESSING

Serves 4

130 g (4¹/₂ oz) green beans

1 Tbsp vegetable oil

WALNUT-MISO DRESSING

60 g (2¹/₄ oz) walnuts

2 Tbsp red miso

4 Tbsp sake

2 Tbsp raw sugar

Prepare walnut-miso dressing. Heat a frying pan over medium heat and add walnuts. Stir constantly for 2-3 minutes until walnuts start to brown. Remove from heat immediately.

Grind toasted walnuts with a *suribachi* or mortar and pestle. In a saucepan over low heat, add miso, sake and sugar. Stir until sugar is dissolved. Add ground walnuts and mix well. Set aside.

Trim ends of green beans and cut into 4-cm (1¹/₂-in) lengths.

Heat oil and stir-fry green beans for about 2 minutes or until tender.

Arrange beans on individual serving plates. Top with walnut-miso dressing and serve.

To vary this recipe, use other types of nuts in place of the walnuts.

When preparing the walnut-miso dressing, turn off the heat once the sugar is dissolved as heat can destroy the beneficial properties of the miso.

Green beans are a popular ingredient in vegetarian diets and feature regularly in *shojin* menus. Here, green beans are stir-fried and flavoured with a dressing of ground walnuts and red miso.

Winter is filled with mystery and beauty.
Just as the cold keeps us indoors,
plants and animals go into hibernation as they
anticipate the start of a whole new cycle of seasons.

冬 Winter

GINGER RICE

Serves 4

220 g (8 oz) Japanese short-grain rice

270 ml (9 fl oz) water

5-cm (2-in) konbu

GINGER SEASONING

30 g (1 oz) ginger

1 tsp Japanese soy sauce

A pinch of sea salt

1 tsp sake

Prepare ginger seasoning. Peel and finely grate ginger, then squeeze grated ginger to extract ginger juice. Mix ginger juice with soy sauce, salt and sake.

Prepare to cook rice according to instructions on page 19. Add ginger seasoning to water for soaking and leave rice to soak for 30 minutes before cooking.

Fluff rice and serve.

Adjust the amount of ginger juice added according to your preference for the intensity of the ginger flavour.

MUSHROOM and VEGETABLE SOUP

Serves 4

1.25 litres (40 fl oz / 5 cups) mushroom dashi (page 20)

$^{1}/_{2}$ tsp sea salt

60 g (2$^{1}/_{4}$ oz) *shungiku* (chrysanthemum) leaves

20 g ($^{2}/_{3}$ oz) enoki mushrooms

80 ml (2$^{1}/_{2}$ fl oz) Japanese soy sauce

80 ml (2$^{1}/_{2}$ fl oz) mirin

10-cm (4-in) konbu

Prepare mushroom dashi. Reserve 2 mushrooms and cut into quarters. Set aside.

Boil a pot of water and add salt. Parboil *shungiku* for about 1 minute, then remove and rinse in cold water. Drain and squeeze gently to remove any excess water. Cut lengthwise into 4 equal portions.

Wash and cut away hard base of enoki mushrooms.

Use a clean damp cloth to wipe the surface of konbu, then add to mushroom dashi. Add soy sauce and mirin and bring to the boil. Lower heat and simmer for 10 minutes.

Arrange mushrooms and *shungiku* in individual serving bowls. Fill bowls with dashi and serve hot.

. . . .

If *shungiku* is not available, substitute with other green vegetables such as spinach or mustard greens.

The hard base of the enoki mushrooms can be used for vegetable tempura (page 104). Clean away the dirt, then coat with batter and deep-fry.

LOTUS ROOT DUMPLINGS

Serves 4

200 g (7 oz) lotus root

320 g (11¼ oz) silken tofu

Shichimi togarashi, to taste

SWEET MISO SAUCE

4 Tbsp sweet miso

2 Tbsp sesame paste

2 Tbsp raw sugar

2 tsp sake

Peel and wash lotus root. Finely grate and place in a fine sieve to drain. Transfer to a bowl.

Mash tofu and mix with grated lotus root.

Divide mixture into 4 equal portions and wrap each portion with muslin cloth, twisting the ends to form a dumpling. Boil muslin bundles in a pot of water for 10 minutes. Remove and unwrap. Place on individual serving plates.

Mix all ingredients for sweet miso sauce. Spoon a little onto each serving plate. Sprinkle with *shichimi togarashi* and serve.

Remove any black spots on the lotus root before grating to ensure that the dumpling will have a smooth, white appearance.

If the sweet miso sauce is too thick, thin it down with a little hot water.

This is one of the first *shojin* dishes I learned to prepare. I was intrigued that the tofu and lotus root could bind without any other agent. These dumplings have a delicate texture and go well with the sweet miso sauce.

WATER CHESTNUT NORI SQUARES

Serves 4

16 water chestnuts

1 sheet nori (seaweed)

Vegetable oil for deep-frying

Wash water chestnuts thoroughly, then peel and finely grate. Place in a fine sieve to drain.

Cut nori into 16 squares. Spread 1 tsp grated water chestnut onto each nori square.

Heat oil for deep-frying. Slip nori squares into hot oil and fry for about 2 minutes or until water chestnut mixture is golden brown. Remove and drain on absorbent paper.

Arrange on individual serving plates and serve immediately.

The grated water chestnuts should not be completely dry before spreading on the nori squares. Squeeze it gently to remove any excess water if necessary.

The liquid from draining the water chestnuts can be served as a refreshing drink.

This dish is simple with some effort required for grating the water chestnuts. The sweetness of the water chestnuts is heightened by deep-frying, and this usually leaves my guests wondering if there was an extra ingredient added.

VEGETABLE ODEN

Serves 4

10-cm (4-in) length daikon

210 g (7$^1/_2$ oz) *age tofu*

100 g (3$^1/_2$ oz) carrot

250 g (9 oz) *konnyaku*

ODEN STOCK

1 litre (32 fl oz / 4 cups) mushroom dashi (page 20)

150 ml (5 fl oz) Japanese soy sauce

150 ml (5 fl oz) mirin

Prepare mushroom dashi. Reserve mushrooms.

Peel and cut daikon into 4 equal rounds, then cut each round into quarters.

Boil a pot of water and add daikon in to cook. Lower the heat and simmer for about 20 minutes or until daikon is tender. Remove and set aside.

Cut *age tofu* into eighths. Peel and cut carrot into bite-size pieces. Drain and rinse *konnyaku*. Cut *konnyaku* into 12 slices.

Prepare *oden* stock. Bring mushroom dashi, soy sauce and mirin to the boil. Add daikon, *age tofu*, carrot, *konnyaku* and mushrooms. Lower heat to medium and simmer for 20 minutes.

Remove ingredients from dashi and arrange in individual serving bowls. Add dashi and serve.

If preferred, enhance the look of the *konnyaku* by twisting it before adding it to the pot. To do this, make a slit in the middle of a slice of *konnyaku* and turn one end into the slit.

Oden is enjoyed during the winter months in Japan
for its hearty mix of ingredients and warming soup stock.
This recipe uses various root vegetables,
mushrooms, tofu and *konnyaku* simmered
in a light mushroom dashi.

MILLET CHAWAN MUSHI

Serves 4

1 fresh yurine (lily bulb)

120 g (4$^1/_3$ oz) millet

500 ml (16 fl oz / 2 cups) water

$^1/_2$ tsp sea salt

SIMMERING STOCK

6 Tbsp mushroom dashi (page 20)

2 Tbsp Japanese soy sauce

2 Tbsp mirin

1 Tbsp raw sugar

CHAWAN MUSHI SAUCE

250 ml (8 fl oz / 1 cup) mushroom dashi (page 20)

$^1/_2$ tsp sea salt

1 tsp Japanese soy sauce

1 Tbsp sake

2 Tbsp *kuzu*

Prepare mushroom dashi. Reserve 2 mushrooms and cut into quarters.

Place ingredients for simmering stock in a saucepan and bring to the boil. Lower heat and add mushroom quarters. Simmer for at least 10 minutes.

Cut base of lily bulb and remove any black spots. Break bulb into petals. Set aside.

Rinse millet briefly and place in a pot with the water and salt. Simmer over low heat for 25 minutes. Turn off heat and let stand for 5 minutes.

Fluff millet with a fork and spoon into 4 tea cups. Top with mushroom quarters and lily bulb petals. Set aside.

Prepare *chawan mushi* sauce. Combine mushroom dashi, salt, soy sauce and sake in a pot and bring to the boil over medium heat. Lower heat to a simmer. Mix *kuzu* with just enough water to form a paste. Add to sauce and whisk to thicken. Spoon sauce into tea cups over millet and serve.

Other vegetables such as gingko nuts and carrot can be added to the *chawan mushi* if desired.

As the millet sits at the base of the tea cups, arrange the vegetables such that the millet remains visible.

Millet is nutritious and has a sweet nutty flavour. The lily bulb petals, mushrooms and gingko nuts add depth to this simple dish.

WINTER SALAD

Serves 4

250 g (9 oz) daikon

60 g (2¼ oz) carrot

1 tsp sea salt

4 pieces *abura-age*

1 Tbsp vegetable oil

ABURA-AGE SAUCE

4 Tbsp mushroom dashi
(page 20)

1 Tbsp raw sugar

1 Tbsp Japanese soy sauce

MUSHROOM SEASONING

1 Tbsp Japanese soy sauce

1 Tbsp raw sugar

SALAD DRESSING

4 Tbsp toasted and ground
sesame seeds (page 21)

1 Tbsp rice vinegar

1 Tbsp Japanese soy sauce

1 Tbsp raw sugar

Prepare mushroom dashi. Reserve mushrooms and cut into fine strips. Set aside.

Peel and julienne daikon and carrot, then toss with salt and let stand for 15 minutes. Rinse off salt and drain well by squeezing daikon and carrot firmly.

Rinse *abura-age* briefly with hot water to remove traces of oil. Squeeze out excess water and cut into fine strips.

Combine ingredients for *abura-age* sauce in a saucepan. Add *abura-age* strips and simmer over medium heat for 3 minutes or until all the liquid is absorbed. Remove and set aside to cool.

Heat oil and stir-fry sliced mushrooms briefly. Add mushroom seasoning and stir-fry for another 2 minutes or until all the liquid is absorbed. Remove and set aside to cool.

In a salad bowl, mix daikon, carrot, *abura-age* and mushrooms. Add ingredients for salad dressing and toss well. Refrigerate for 2–3 hours before serving.

Arrange on individual serving dishes and serve at room temperature.

This dish can be prepared several days ahead as it will keep for up to 1 week in the refrigerator. The flavour improves if left to sit for at least 2 days.

This dish always reminds me of *yusheng*,
the colourful salad served during the Lunar New Year.
This winter salad has a more subtle mix of colours
and a lovely crunchy texture from the daikon and carrot.

GINGER RICE

Serves 4

220 g (8 oz) Japanese short-grain rice

270 ml (9 fl oz) water

5-cm (2-in) konbu

GINGER SEASONING

30 g (1 oz) ginger

1 tsp Japanese soy sauce

A pinch of sea salt

1 tsp sake

Prepare ginger seasoning. Peel and finely grate ginger, then squeeze grated ginger to extract ginger juice. Mix ginger juice with soy sauce, salt and sake.

Prepare to cook rice according to instructions on page 19. Add ginger seasoning to water for soaking and leave rice to soak for 30 minutes before cooking.

Fluff rice and serve.

....

Adjust the amount of ginger juice added according to your preference for the intensity of the ginger flavour.

Note: The ginger rice and mushrooms and vegetable soup recipes have been reproduced from pages 118 and 119 for completeness and easy reference.

MUSHROOM and VEGETABLE SOUP

Serves 4

1.25 litres (40 fl oz / 5 cups) mushroom dashi (page 20)

1/2 tsp sea salt

60 g (2 1/4 oz) *shungiku* (chrysanthemum) leaves

20 g (2/3 oz) enoki mushrooms

80 ml (2 1/2 fl oz) Japanese soy sauce

80 ml (2 1/2 fl oz) mirin

10-cm (4-in) konbu

Prepare mushroom dashi. Reserve 2 mushrooms and cut into quarters. Set aside.

Boil a pot of water and add salt. Parboil *shungiku* for about 1 minute, then remove and rinse in cold water. Drain and squeeze gently to remove any excess water. Cut lengthwise into 4 equal portions.

Wash and cut away hard base of enoki mushrooms.

Use a clean damp cloth to wipe the surface of konbu, then add to mushroom dashi. Add soy sauce and mirin and bring to the boil. Lower heat and simmer for 10 minutes.

Arrange mushrooms and *shungiku* in individual serving bowls. Fill bowls with dashi and serve hot.

. . . .

If *shungiku* is not available, substitute with other green vegetables such as spinach or mustard greens.

The hard base of the enoki mushrooms can be used for vegetable tempura (page 104). Clean away the dirt, then coat with batter and deep-fry.

DAIKON with MISO

Serves 4

12-cm (5-in) length daikon

Rice water, as needed

4 tsp sweet miso

2 tsp sake

1 tsp raw sugar

Peel and cut daikon to 4 equal rounds.

Boil a pot of rice water and add daikon. Lower heat and simmer for about 20 minutes or until daikon is tender.

Mix the miso, sake and sugar in a saucepan over low heat. Turn off heat when sugar is dissolved.

Cut each daikon round into quarters and spread with miso sauce. Arrange on individual serving plates and serve.

For an additional depth of flavour, add some finely grated yuzu rind to the miso sauce.

Known as *furofuki daikon*, this is commonly prepared in Japan in the winter, when the daikons are large and plump. The daikon is boiled in rice water which helps to bring out its natural sweetness.

BRAISED GOBO

Serves 4

25-cm (10-in) length burdock (*gobo*)

500 ml (16 fl oz / 2 cups) konbu dashi (page 19)

1 Tbsp sugar

1 Tbsp Japanese soy sauce

2 Tbsp sake

$1/2$ tsp sea salt

Peel burdock, then cut at a 45 degree angle to get 12 pieces, each about 2-cm ($3/4$-in) long. Soak immediately in water to avoid discolouration. Drain before using.

Prepare konbu dashi. Add sugar, soy sauce, sake and salt. Bring to the boil and add burdock. Boil for 10 minutes, then lower heat and simmer for about 20 minutes. Remove burdock and leave to cool.

Slice each piece of burdock into half along its length. Arrange the two halves in a V shape. Place three sets on each serving plate, drizzle with some simmering liquid and serve.

....

To enhance the visual appeal of this dish, choose a length of burdock that has an even thickness.

This recipe offers another way of preparing the
nourishing burdock, known in Japanese as *gobo*.
This interesting presentation is meant to symbolise arrows
that pierce through a person's heart to remove all evil.

TOFU STEAK

Serves 4

160 g (5²/₃ oz) red capsicum (bell pepper)

Olive oil, as needed

20 g (²/₃ oz) ginger

320 g (11¼ oz) *momen* tofu

¹/₂ tsp sea salt

40 g (1¹/₃ oz) breadcrumbs

50 g (1³/₄ oz) black sesame seeds

50 g (1³/₄ oz) white sesame seeds

4 Tbsp Japanese soy sauce

3 Tbsp mirin

2 Tbsp vegetable oil

Brush capsicum with olive oil. Place under a hot grill for 10 minutes or until the skin is a bit charred. Turn and grill other side for 5 minutes. Remove from grill and set aside to cool. When capsicum is cool, remove and discard stem. Peel off and discard skin. Place flesh and 1 tsp olive oil in a blender and process into a purée.

Peel and finely grate ginger. Squeeze pulp for juice and set juice and pulp aside separately.

Rinse *momen* tofu and crumble into small pieces using hands. Mix tofu with salt, breadcrumbs, capsicum purée and grated ginger pulp. Divide into 4 equal portions and shape into oval patties. Let sit for about 30 minutes.

Mix white and black sesame seeds together. Coat patties with sesame seeds.

Heat vegetable oil in a pan over medium heat. Add patties and pan-fry for about 4 minutes on each side.

Mix ginger juice with soy sauce and mirin.

Arrange patties on individual serving plates and serve with ginger-mirin sauce.

....

Letting the patties sit for about 30 minutes will allow the breadcrumbs to absorb moisture from the mixture and be more flavourful. If the patties are too soft to shape, add breadcrumbs gradually until it is firm enough to shape.

The mixture of the red capsicum and tofu resembles that of salmon, and these patties are sometimes referred to as tofu-salmon steaks.

NAGAIMO and ORANGE SALAD

Serves 4

1¹/₂ medium oranges,
about 375 g (13¹/₄ oz)

250 g (9 oz) *nagaimo*

100 g (3¹/₂ oz) tomato

100 g (3¹/₂ oz) broccoli

SALAD DRESSING

¹/₂ medium orange,
about 125 g (4¹/₂ oz)

2 Tbsp mirin

2 Tbsp rice vinegar

1 Tbsp raw sugar

1 Tbsp Japanese soy sauce

¹/₂ tsp sesame oil

Prepare salad dressing. Extract the juice from the orange half and strain to remove any pulp and seeds. Measure out 50 ml (1²/₃ fl oz) orange juice and mix with mirin, vinegar, sugar, soy sauce and sesame oil. Set aside.

Peel oranges and break into chunks. Peel and cut *nagaimo* into chunks. Cut tomato into 8 wedges.

Trim broccoli and cut out 4 florets. Boil a pot of water and cook broccoli for 3 minutes. Remove and plunge into cold water.

Divide orange and *nagaimo* chunks, tomato wedges and broccoli among 4 individual serving plates. Drizzle with salad dressing and serve.

Plunging the broccoli into cold water will stop the cooking process, thus retaining the fresh green colour and texture of the broccoli.

This salad features a variety of ingredients of different colours, making it visually pleasing, especially during winter when the dishes are usually not as brightly coloured.

LOTUS ROOT with AZUKI BEANS

Serves 4

100 g (3½ oz) azuki beans

20-cm (8-in) length
lotus root

SIMMERING STOCK

500 ml (16 fl oz / 2 cups)
konbu dashi (page 19)

4 tsp Japanese soy sauce

4 tsp mirin

4 tsp sake

Rinse and soak azuki beans for 1 hour. Boil a pot of water (at least 500 ml / 16 fl oz / 2 cups) and add azuki beans. Boil for 1 hour or until beans are tender. Drain and set aside.

Wash and peel lotus root. Slice into 0.5-cm (¼-in) thick slices.

Prepare konbu dashi. Add soy sauce, mirin and sake and bring to the boil.

Add lotus root, lower heat and simmer for 10 minutes. Add azuki beans and simmer for another 5 minutes.

Remove and arrange lotus root and azuki beans on individual serving plates. Serve.

Lotus root discolours easily when it is peeled and cut. To avoid this, soak sliced lotus root in water mixed with 1–2 Tbsp vinegar.

Soaking the azuki beans will help reduce the cooking time. Without soaking, the azuki beans may take 1½–2 hours to cook.

The cylindrical air chambers in lotus root resemble
binochulars and symbolise foresight to the Japanese.
The sweetness of the azuki beans compliments
the flavour of the lotus root, making this an unusual dish
suitable even for serving on special occasions.

Desserts

In the Zen tradition, desserts are not usually
included with the meal, although a simple dish of
seasonal fruits may be served. Desserts are typically
reserved for special occasions such as the tea ceremony,
but it would also be simple. In this section,
I have included a dessert for each season
to complete the dining experience.

MOCHI BALLS
(Spring)

Serves 4

90 g (3¹/₄ oz) glutinous rice flour

155 g (5¹/₂ oz) silken tofu

BLACK SESAME SAUCE

4 Tbsp black sesame paste

2 Tbsp hot water

2 Tbsp maple syrup

Knead rice flour and silken tofu together to get a firm dough. Roll into small balls.

Boil a pot of water and add mochi balls. Boil for about 3 minutes or until balls float to the surface. Drain and place mochi balls into a bowl of cold water to cool.

Prepare black sesame sauce. Mix black sesame paste, hot water and maple syrup and blend well.

Drain mochi balls and arrange on individual serving plates. Serve with black sesame sauce.

WATERMELON JELLY
(Summer)

Serves 4

3 g ($^1/_{10}$ oz) *kanten* powder

300 ml (10 fl oz / 1$^1/_4$ cups) watermelon juice

Mix *kanten* powder with 5 tsp watermelon juice.

Pour 100 ml (3$^1/_2$ fl oz) watermelon juice in a saucepan and bring to the boil. Remove from heat. Stir in *kanten* mixture, followed by remaining juice.

Pour mixture into a 17.5 x 8 x 6-cm (7 x 3 x 2$^1/_3$-in) metal tray. Cover and refrigerate for about 1 hour or until jelly is set.

Cut the watermelon jelly into cubes and arrange on individual serving plates. Garnish as desired.

Taste the watermelon before using it to make this jelly. If it is not sweet enough, add some sugar syrup or a natural sweetener to sweeten it to taste.

SWEET POTATO WAGASHI (Autumn)

Serves 4

400 g (14 1/3 oz) Japanese sweet potatoes

2 Tbsp raw sugar

A pinch of salt

1 Tbsp red bean paste

1/2 tsp matcha powder

Wash and cut sweet potatoes into rounds. Bring a pot of water to the boil, then lower heat to a simmer. Add sweet potatoes and simmer for 10–20 minutes or until sweet potatoes are tender. Drain and set aside to cool before peeling.

Place a pan over low heat. Add peeled sweet potatoes and mash in the pan. This will help to remove excess liquid from the sweet potatoes. Add sugar and salt and mix well.

Set 1 Tbsp of the sweet potato mash aside. Divide the remaining mash into equal portions. Place each portion on a sheet of plastic wrap and twist the wrap to shape the mash into a firm ball.

Add a dab of red bean paste to the tip of each sweet potato ball.

Mix the reserved mash with matcha powder until it is evenly coloured. Add a dab of green mash to the tip of each ball as well.

Arrange the sweet potato *wagashi* on individual serving plates and serve.

Some practice may be necessary to form the sweet potato mash into a presentable shape. Dab the red bean paste and green mash on the side of the balls for an artistic presentation. You may also reshape the dumplings after dabbing with the red bean paste or green mash so the coloured mash is incorporated into the ball.

POACHED PEARS (Winter)

Serves 4

2 firm, ripe Packham pears, each about 200 (7 oz)

750 ml (24 fl oz / 3 cups) red wine

4 Tbsp maple syrup

Natural sweetener or raw sugar, to taste

Peel and cut the pears into bite-size pieces.

Place the red wine, maple syrup and pears in a saucepan. Cook over low heat for 15–20 minutes until the pears are translucent. Add natural sweetener or raw sugar to taste.

Remove from heat and let cool at room temperature. Refrigerate for 1 hour.

Serve poached pears in individual serving bowls.

The red wine should cover the pears completely. To minimise the amount of red wine required, use a small saucepan.

Glossary

Fresh Ingredients

01 Bamboo Shoot
This is the tender young shoot of the bamboo plant and it is usually available in spring and in the early summer. More work is required to prepare fresh bamboo shoot, but canned or vacuum-packed bamboo shoot are now easily available. These cream coloured shoots are commonly used in Asian cooking and are enjoyed for their crunchy texture and mild sweet flavour. Bamboo groves are common in the Zen temples and as such, the use of bamboo shoot in shojin cooking is a natural use of this food resource.

02 Burdock (Gobo)
Burdock is a root that is said to have many health benefits. It turns dark quickly when cut and as such, soak the cut burdock in water to avoid discolouration. This will also help remove any bitterness from the root. Choose burdock that is firm. Wrap in wet paper towels and store in a plastic bag in the refrigerator.

03 Daikon
Daikon, also known as white radish, is a member of the radish family and the white coloured root is especially large and succulent during winter. Although the leaves are edible, they are often removed when sold in the stores as the leaves turn yellow quite easily. Daikon is known to aid digestion and promote respiratory health. It is widely used in Japanese cooking.

04 Edamame
Edamame beans are soy beans that are still green and unripe in their pods. They are in season from summer to the early autumn. Boiled edamame beans are commonly available as a side dish in Japanese restaurants. Fresh or frozen edamame beans are easily available from supermarkets. Edamame beans are enjoyed for their light, sweet flavour.

05 Green Shiso
Green shiso or perilla is generally cultivated for use all year round. It is also known as Japanese basil, as it has a remarkable fragrance and is often used as a garnish in sashimi dishes, or in salads and tempura.

06 Japanese Cucumber
Although cucumber season is in summer, cucumbers are now available all year round. The Japanese cucumber is less watery and has a firmer texture than regular cucumbers. It is also generally shorter and more slender compared with other varieties. The Japanese cucumber is enjoyed for its crunchy texture and sweet flavour.

07 Japanese Eggplant (Nasu)
There are many different varieties of eggplant, but the Japanese eggplant or *nasu* is usually sweeter than the others. Japanese eggplant has deep purple coloured skin and firm flesh and is usually about 10–15-cm (4–6-in) long. Choose Japanese eggplant with a firm and shiny appearance and no obvious blemishes.

01

02

03

04

05

07

06

08 Japanese Pumpkin

A member of the squash family, the Japanese pumpkin or *kabocha* is slightly sweeter than other varieties of squash. It has rich yellow coloured flesh and dark green skin. The skin of the pumpkin is edible except that it may be a bit tough if it is too thick. If so, thin the skin by peeling with a vegetable peeler.

09 Japanese Sweet Potatoes

Japanese sweet potato or *satsumaimo* season is in autumn. These tuberous roots have a purplish red skin and whitish yellow flesh. Although largely similar to other types of sweet potato, Japanese sweet potatoes are sweeter and have a softer texture. Good quality Japanese sweet potatoes do not discolour easily when cut.

10 Lotus Root

Lotus root or renkon is typically harvested in winter. The root is characterised by air chambers that run through its length and which create a pretty flower-like pattern when sliced crosswise. Choose lotus root that is thick, beige-white in colour and without blemishes.

11 Mountain Yam

Yamatoimo (11a) and *nagaimo* (11b) are different types of tuber belonging to the Dioscorea family. Both *yamatoimo* and *nagaimo* are cylindrical in shape except that *yamatoimo* is fan-shaped at one end. *Yamatoimo* has a dense and powdery texture while *nagaimo* is crunchy and more watery. When selecting either yam, choose those that have a smooth flawless surface without any bruises.

Wrap in wet paper towels and store in a plastic bag in the refrigerator. Those with sensitive skin may experience itchiness when handling these yams. Wear gloves to avoid this. Soothe the affected area with vinegar or lemon juice.

12 Mushrooms, Enoki

These white coloured mushrooms have tiny caps and slender stems. They grow in tight clusters and are widely cultivated and hence easily available all year round. Enoki mushrooms can be eaten raw. Choose clusters that look fresh and are firm and crisp. Cut off the base before using.

13 Mushrooms, Nameko

Nameko mushrooms have a faintly sweet and nutty flavour. They grow in clusters and have orange-brown caps and white stems. The fresh mushrooms have a shiny coating on their caps, making them feel slippery to the touch. Popularly used in Japanese cooking, *nameko* mushrooms are widely cultivated and are more readily available in cans or in vacuum-packs as fresh *nameko* has a very short shelf life.

14 *Shungiku* (Chrysanthemum Leaves)

Part of the chrysanthemum family, these greens are enjoyed as a vegetable in Japan. The *shungiku* is similar to another vegetable, *tong hao*, which is commonly used when serving steamboat in Asia. Compared to *tong hao*, Japanese *shungiku* has a more defined leaf pattern and a stronger fragrance. It is best eaten raw or very lightly cooked.

08

09

10

11a

11b

12

13

14

Tofu

Tofu is made by coagulating soy milk and moulding the resulting curd into blocks. As it is rich in protein, tofu plays an important part in the vegetarian diet. There are several varieties of tofu and a few are used in the recipes in this book.

15 Abura-age

Abura-age is a deep-fried tofu pocket or skin. It is made by deep-frying thin slices of tofu, during which an air pocket naturally forms. *Abura-age* is popularly stuffed, but it can also be sliced and added to soups and stir-fries.

16 Astuage

Atsuage is a thick, deep-fried tofu. Large blocks of fresh tofu are deep-fried until golden brown, giving the *astuage* a crisp coating, while the tofu remains soft and smooth inside.

17 Momen Tofu

Momen tofu is also known as regular tofu. It has a firm texture that makes it easy to be picked up using chopsticks. In making *momen* tofu, cotton cloth is used to drain the curd, leaving a distinctive mark of the fabric on the blocks of tofu.

18 Silken Tofu

Silken tofu has a fine and delicate texture. It is produced by coagulating soy milk without curdling it. Traditionally, in Japanese cuisine, silken tofu is cut into delicate cubes to display the culinary knife skill of the chef. However, in shojin cooking, silken tofu is sometimes crumbled into pieces to express equanimity.

19 Water Chestnuts

Water chestnuts grow underwater in the mud, hence fresh water chestnuts sometimes still have traces of mud on them. These small bulb-like vegetables have a thin, brownish-black skin and white, crunchy flesh. Water chestnuts are available in cans or in vacuum packs and are a convenient option, but it is best to use fresh water chestnuts if available, as they are far superior in taste. Choose water chestnuts that are firm with no blemishes.

20 Yurine (Lily Bulb)

Yurine, the edible bulb of certain lily plants, is available during autumn in Japan and China. Outside of Japan and China, yurine is mostly found in packets although fresh yurine, imported from Japan, may sometimes be available. The creamy white bulbs separate into multiple segments when cut. Yurine has a mild, sweet flavour and a crunchy texture.

15

16

17

18

19

20

Dry Ingredients

01 Azuki Beans

Azuki beans are possibly the most common Japanese variety of beans outside of Japan. It is regarded as a health food as it is high in protein, fibre and vitamins. Cooked azuki beans have a sweet aroma and is a popular ingredient used in Japanese breads, cakes and desserts.

02 Gingko Nuts

Gingko nuts have a mild flavour with a hint of bitterness. The season for gingko nuts is autumn in Japan. If fresh gingko nuts are available, choose those that are large and white. Alternatively, shelled gingko nuts sold in packets are easily available in Asian food stores.

03 Hijiki

Hijiki is a dark coloured seaweed that is high in vitamins and minerals. It is said that the regular consumption of *hijiki* can contribute to a full head of dark, lustrous hair. Dried *hijiki* is sold in packet form and is widely available in Asian food stores. Rinse *hijiki* well to remove dirt, then reconstitute in water before use.

04 Kanten

Kanten is made from tengusa seaweed that is high in fibre and contains zero calories. It is used for its gelling properties and is an excellent option for vegetarians who cannot use animal gelatin. *Kanten* is available in stick and powder form.

05 Katakuriko

Katakuriko is a starch originally derived from *katakuri* roots. However, it is commonly made from sweet potatoes or potatoes today due to the scarcity of *katakuri* roots. It can be used as a gluten-free substitute for plain (all-purpose) flour and as a thickening agent.

06 Konbu

Konbu is a type of seaweed that is essential in Japanese cooking. It is rich in amino acid, iodine and calcium and is widely used to make stock. When choosing konbu, choose pieces that are thick and broad. Wipe the surface with a clean, damp cloth before using. Do not wash, as the white powder on the seaweed is the natural salt that contributes to the flavour.

07 Konnyaku

Konnyaku is a firm jelly made from the root of the devil's tongue. It has little taste of its own and is enjoyed mainly for its texture. *Konnyaku* is high in fibre and rich in minerals, and is consumed as a therapeutic food by Buddhist monks in Japan. *Konnyaku* is now also widely used in Japanese cooking.

08 Kuzu

A member of the legume family, *kuzu* is known for its medicinal properties, especially for treating digestive ailments. The starch derived from the *kuzu* root gives food a good elasticity, and it is often used to make sesame 'tofu' in *shojin* cooking.

09 Millet

Millet is a tiny yellow grain of the rice family. Interest in millet seems to have grown in recent years as it offers a gluten-free option to flour made from wheat. Millet is nutritious and high in fibre. It is also highly alkaline which makes it easy on our stomachs.

10 Sesame Seeds

Both black and white sesame seeds are commonly used in Japanese cooking. These tiny teardrop shape seeds are rich in oil, protein and minerals. Sesame seeds have a distinctive nutty aroma when toasted and ground.